FAVORITE BRAND NAME™

Easy Weeknight Meals *in 30 Minutes or Less*

Publications International, Ltd.

Favorite Brand Name Recipes at www.fbnr.com

Microwave Cooking: Microwave ovens vary in wattage. Use the cooking times as guidelines and check for doneness before adding more time.

Preparation/Cooking Times: Preparation times are based on the approximate amount of time required to assemble the recipe before cooking, baking, chilling or serving. These times include preparation steps such as measuring, chopping and mixing. The fact that some preparations and cooking can be done simultaneously is taken into account. Preparation of optional ingredients and serving suggestions is not included.

Table of Contents

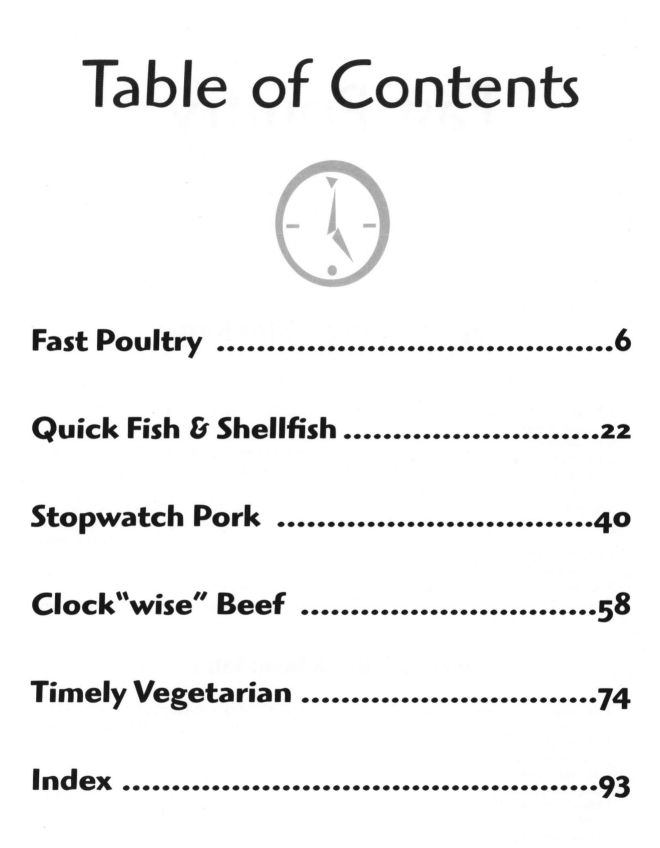

Fast Poultry

Spicy Mango Chicken

Prep: 15 minutes   **Cook:** 15 minutes

Mango & Black Bean Salsa
(recipe follows)
¼ cup mango nectar
¼ cup chopped fresh cilantro
2 jalapeño chile peppers, seeded
 and finely chopped
2 teaspoons vegetable oil
2 teaspoons LAWRY'S®
 Seasoned Salt
½ teaspoon LAWRY'S® Garlic
 Powder with Parsley
½ teaspoon ground cumin
4 boneless, skinless chicken
 breasts (about 1 pound)

Prepare Mango & Black Bean Salsa.

In small bowl, combine all ingredients except chicken and salsa; mix well. Brush marinade on both sides of chicken. Grill or broil chicken 10 to 15 minutes or until chicken is thoroughly cooked, turning once and basting often with additional marinade. *Do not baste during last 5 minutes of cooking.* Discard any remaining marinade. Top chicken with Mango & Black Bean Salsa.   *Makes 4 servings*

Hint: Jalapeño peppers can sting and irritate the skin; wear rubber gloves when handling peppers and do not touch eyes.

Mango & Black Bean Salsa

1 ripe mango, peeled, seeded and
 chopped
1 cup canned black beans, rinsed
 and drained
½ cup chopped tomato
2 thinly sliced green onions
1 tablespoon chopped fresh
 cilantro
1½ teaspoons lime juice
1½ teaspoons red wine vinegar
½ teaspoon LAWRY'S®
 Seasoned Salt

In medium bowl, combine all ingredients; mix well. Let stand 25 minutes to allow flavors to blend.   *Makes about 2¾ cups*

Spicy Mango Chicken

Turkey Tostadas

Prep and Cook Time: 20 minutes

1 package BUTTERBALL® Fresh
   Boneless Turkey Breast Strips
1 tablespoon vegetable oil
1 tablespoon chili powder
½ teaspoon salt
8 (6-inch) tostadas or corn tortillas
1 cup fat free vegetarian
   refried beans
2 cups shredded iceberg lettuce
1 cup (4 ounces) shredded low fat
   Cheddar cheese
1 avocado, coarsely chopped
1 cup chopped tomato
½ cup chopped green onions

Heat oil in large nonstick skillet over medium heat until hot. Add turkey strips; sprinkle with chili powder and salt. Cook and stir frequently about 5 minutes or until no longer pink. Spread each tostada with 2 tablespoons refried beans. Divide shredded lettuce evenly among tostadas. Place cooked turkey strips on top of lettuce; sprinkle with cheese. Add avocado, tomato and onions to each tostada. Serve with low fat sour cream and salsa, if desired. *Makes 8 tostadas*

Tip: To assure safe, tender, juicy fresh cuts, cook turkey until no longer pink in center, being careful not to overcook.

Chicken and Asparagus Salad

Prep Time: 10 minutes   **Cook Time:** 4 minutes

½ cup HELLMANN'S® or BEST
   FOODS® Real Mayonnaise
½ cup sour cream or plain yogurt
¼ cup thinly sliced green onions
1 tablespoon chopped fresh basil
   or ½ teaspoon dried basil
   leaves, crushed
1 tablespoon lemon juice
½ teaspoon salt
¼ teaspoon grated lemon peel
   (optional)
12 ounces asparagus
8 cups torn mixed salad greens
2½ cups cubed cooked chicken
   (about 1 pound)
1 cup cherry tomatoes or yellow or
   red grape tomatoes, halved

In small bowl, combine mayonnaise, sour cream, green onions, basil, lemon juice, salt and lemon peel. Cover and chill to blend flavors until ready to serve.

In medium skillet, bring ½ cup water to a boil. Add asparagus; cover and cook 4 minutes or until crisp-tender. Drain and rinse with cold water until completely cool.

In large salad bowl, combine greens, chicken and tomatoes. Arrange salad mixture on plates; top with asparagus. To serve, spoon dressing over each salad. *Makes 4 servings*

Santa Fe Spaghetti

Prep and Cook Time: 20 minutes

8 ounces uncooked thin spaghetti
or vermicelli
1 tablespoon vegetable oil
12 ounces boneless chicken or
turkey, cut into 1-inch cubes
1½ teaspoons minced garlic
1 teaspoon ground cumin
1 teaspoon ground coriander
¼ teaspoon salt
⅛ teaspoon black pepper
1 package (16 ounces) frozen bell
pepper and onion strips for
stir-fry, thawed
1½ cups prepared salsa or
picante sauce
½ cup sour cream
1½ teaspoons cornstarch
1 tablespoon chopped fresh
cilantro or parsley

1. Cook spaghetti according to package directions.

2. Meanwhile, heat oil in large, deep skillet over medium-high heat until hot. Add chicken and garlic. Sprinkle with cumin, coriander, salt and black pepper; stir-fry 2 minutes.

3. Stir in bell peppers and onions and salsa; cook over medium heat 4 minutes. Combine sour cream and cornstarch in small bowl; mix well. Stir into chicken mixture; cook 2 to 3 minutes or until sauce has thickened and chicken is no longer pink in center, stirring occasionally.

4. Drain spaghetti; serve with chicken mixture. Sprinkle with cilantro.

Makes 4 servings

Classic Turkey Parmesan

Prep Time: 15 minutes   **Cook Time:** 15 minutes

2 eggs
2 tablespoons milk or water
1 cup Italian-seasoned dry bread
crumbs
¼ cup all-purpose flour
½ teaspoon salt
¼ teaspoon freshly ground black
pepper
1 package JENNIE-O TURKEY
STORE® Turkey Breast Slices
2 to 4 tablespoons olive oil,
as needed
3 cloves garlic, peeled, halved
1½ cups prepared spaghetti sauce
or spicy spaghetti sauce
1½ cups (6 ounces) shredded
mozzarella cheese
¼ cup grated Parmesan cheese
Chopped fresh basil (optional)

Heat oven to 350°F. Beat together eggs and milk in shallow pie plate or dish; place bread crumbs in another pie plate. Combine flour, salt and pepper in plastic or paper bag. Add turkey slices to bag one at a time; shake to coat lightly with seasoned flour. Dip in egg mixture, letting excess drip off; roll in crumbs to coat lightly. Heat 2 tablespoons oil in large non-stick skillet over medium heat. Add garlic cloves; cook 1 minute. Push garlic to edges of skillet. Add turkey slices to skillet in batches (do not crowd); cook 3 minutes per side or until golden brown and no longer pink in center. Transfer turkey as it is cooked to 13×9-inch baking dish. Repeat with remaining turkey adding additional oil to pan as necessary. Discard garlic; add spaghetti sauce to same skillet. Simmer 2 minutes or until heated through. Spoon over turkey; top with mozzarella and Parmesan cheeses. Bake about 12 minutes or until turkey is hot and cheese has melted. Sprinkle with basil, if desired.

Makes 6 servings

Thai Chicken Pizza

Prep and Cook Time: 25 minutes

2 boneless skinless chicken breast
　　halves (½ pound)
2 teaspoons Thai seasoning
　　Nonstick cooking spray
2 tablespoons pineapple juice
1 tablespoon peanut butter
1 tablespoon oyster sauce
1 teaspoon Thai chili paste*
2 (10-inch) flour tortillas
½ cup shredded carrot
½ cup sliced green onions
½ cup red bell pepper slices
¼ cup chopped fresh cilantro
½ cup (2 ounces) shredded
　　part-skim mozzarella cheese

*Thai chili paste is available at
some larger supermarkets and at
Oriental markets.*

1. Preheat oven to 400°F. Cut chicken breasts crosswise into thin 1½×½-inch slices. Sprinkle with Thai seasoning. Let stand 5 minutes. Spray large nonstick skillet with cooking spray; heat over medium heat until hot. Add chicken. Cook and stir 3 minutes or until chicken is lightly browned and no longer pink in center.

2. Combine pineapple juice, peanut butter, oyster sauce and chili paste in small bowl until smooth. Place tortillas on baking sheets. Spread peanut butter mixture over tortillas. Divide chicken, carrot, onion, pepper and cilantro evenly between each tortilla. Sprinkle with cheese. Bake 5 minutes or until tortillas are crisp and cheese is melted. Cut into wedges.

Makes 4 servings

Mexican Style Skillet

Prep Time: 5 minutes　　**Total Time:** 15 minutes

1¾ cups water
1 (16-ounce) jar salsa
2 teaspoons HERB-OX® chicken
　　flavored instant bouillon
　　& seasoning
1½ cups instant rice, uncooked
1 (11-ounce) can whole kernel
　　corn with diced bell peppers
1 (4¼-ounce) jar diced green
　　chilies
1 (10-ounce) can HORMEL® chunk
　　breast of chicken
1 cup shredded Monterey Jack
　　& Cheddar cheese blend
Tortilla chips, for garnish
Additional toppings such as
　　salsa, sour cream and
　　guacamole

In large nonstick skillet, combine water, salsa and bouillon. Bring mixture to a boil. Stir in rice, corn and green chilies. Top with chicken and cheese. Cover and remove from heat; let stand for 5 minutes. If desired, garnish with tortilla chips and serve with additional salsa, sour cream and guacamole.

Makes 6 to 8 servings

Easy Italian-Style Chicken

Prep and Cook Time: 20 minutes

4 cups (6 ounces) wide egg
　　noodles, uncooked
1 tablespoon olive oil
12 ounces boneless chicken, cut
　　into 1-inch cubes
1 tablespoon paprika
1 teaspoon dried thyme leaves
½ teaspoon salt
⅛ teaspoon black pepper
1 cup chopped onion
1 medium green bell pepper,
　　chopped
1 tablespoon bottled minced garlic
2 cans (14½ ounces each)
　　chunky-style diced tomatoes
　　or pasta-ready diced
　　tomatoes, undrained
1 can (about 14 ounces)
　　chicken broth
1½ cups sliced button mushrooms
¼ cup half-and-half or whipping
　　cream

1. Cook noodles according to package directions.

2. Meanwhile, heat oil in large saucepan over medium-high heat until hot. Add chicken; sprinkle with paprika, thyme, salt and black pepper. Cook and stir 1 minute. Add onion, bell pepper and garlic; cook 2 minutes, stirring occasionally.

3. Add tomatoes with juice, broth and mushrooms. Cover; bring to a boil over high heat. Reduce heat to medium-low; cook, covered, 2 minutes. Stir in half-and-half; cook 1 minute or until heated through.

4. Drain noodles; transfer to 4 shallow serving bowls. Ladle chicken mixture over noodles. *Makes 4 servings*

Golden Risotto with Turkey & Asparagus

Prep Time: 15 minutes　　　**Cook Time:** 15 minutes

1 package JENNIE-O TURKEY
　　STORE® Turkey Breast or
　　Smoked Turkey Sausage, cut
　　into 1-inch diagonal slices
½ cup minced onion
1 tablespoon butter
1 tablespoon CARAPELLI® olive oil
1 cup arborio or California
　　medium-grain rice
1 pinch saffron threads
4½ cups hot chicken broth
1 pound asparagus, green beans
　　or peas cut into 1-inch
　　lengths, blanched
½ cup grated Parmesan cheese
　　Chopped chives

In large saucepan, sauté onion in butter and olive oil 2 minutes or until tender. Stir in rice until evenly coated. Add saffron to broth. Add 1 cup broth to rice. Stir until liquid is absorbed. Continue to add broth, 1 cup at a time, until all liquid is absorbed, about 10 minutes. Stir in asparagus, turkey and cheese. Sprinkle with chopped chives. *Makes 4 servings*

Chicken Tostadas

Prep and Cook Time: 28 minutes

6 (8-inch) flour tortillas
Nonstick cooking spray
1 can (15 ounces) black beans,
    rinsed and drained
½ cup hot salsa
2 teaspoons chili powder, divided
1 teaspoon ground cumin, divided
12 ounces chicken tenders
2 cups finely chopped tomatoes,
    well drained
1 cup chopped onion
1½ cups (6 ounces) shredded
    Cheddar cheese
2 cups shredded romaine or
    iceberg lettuce
Sour cream (optional)

1. Preheat oven to 350°F. Place tortillas on two large baking sheets, overlapping as little as possible. Spray both sides of tortillas with nonstick cooking spray. Bake 7 minutes. Turn tortillas over and bake 3 minutes more or until no longer soft and flexible.

2. While tortillas are baking, place beans in food processor and process until smooth. Transfer to medium saucepan. Stir in salsa, 1 teaspoon chili powder and ½ teaspoon cumin; bring to a boil over medium heat.

3. Cut chicken into ½-inch pieces. Sprinkle with remaining 1 teaspoon chili powder and ½ teaspoon cumin. Coat large nonstick skillet with cooking spray; heat over medium heat. Add chicken; cook and stir 5 minutes or until cooked through.

4. Spread bean mixture on tortillas to within ½ inch of edges. Top with chicken, tomatoes, onion and cheese. Bake 2 minutes or just until cheese is melted. Top with lettuce and sour cream, if desired. Serve immediately.   *Makes 6 servings*

Glazed Chicken, Carrots and Celery

Prep and Cook Time: 23 minutes

1 cup uncooked rice
1 teaspoon dried dill weed
1 teaspoon dried parsley flakes
½ teaspoon salt
¼ teaspoon black pepper
1 pound chicken tenders
1 tablespoon vegetable oil
3 ribs celery, thinly sliced
2 carrots, thinly sliced
1 cup apple juice
1 chicken bouillon cube
Fresh sage leaves

1. Cook rice according to package directions.

2. Meanwhile, mix dill, parsley, salt and pepper in medium bowl. Add chicken tenders; toss to coat.

3. Heat oil in nonstick skillet over medium heat. Add chicken, celery and carrots; cook and stir about 5 minutes or until chicken is tender.

4. Stir in apple juice and bouillon cube. Cook and stir over high heat about 10 minutes or until liquid has thickened and reduced to about 2 tablespoons. Serve over rice. Garnish with sage leaves.   *Makes 4 servings*

Turkey Tetrazzini with Roasted Red Peppers

Prep and Cook Time: 20 minutes

6 ounces uncooked egg noodles
3 tablespoons butter
¼ cup all-purpose flour
1 can (14½ ounces) chicken broth
1 cup whipping cream
2 tablespoons dry sherry
2 cans (6 ounces each) sliced
   mushrooms, drained
1 jar (7½ ounces) roasted red
   peppers, drained and cut into
   ½-inch strips
2 cups chopped cooked turkey
1 teaspoon Italian seasoning
½ cup grated Parmesan cheese

1. Cook egg noodles in large saucepan according to package directions. Drain well; return noodles to saucepan.

2. While noodles are cooking, melt butter in medium saucepan over medium heat. Add flour; whisk until smooth. Add broth; bring to a boil over high heat. Remove from heat. Gradually add whipping cream and sherry; stir to combine.

3. Add mushrooms and peppers to noodles; toss to combine. Add half of broth mixture to noodle mixture. Combine remaining chicken broth mixture, turkey and Italian seasoning in large bowl.

4. Spoon noodle mixture into serving dish. Make a well in center of noodles and spoon in turkey mixture. Sprinkle cheese over top.

Makes 6 servings

Cacciatore Pineapple Chicken

Prep: 10 minutes   **Cook:** 15 minutes

1 can (20 ounces) DOLE®
   Pineapple Chunks
4 boneless, skinless chicken breast
   halves
1 teaspoon garlic powder
1 teaspoon vegetable or olive oil
1 medium onion, thinly sliced
1 tablespoon dried oregano leaves
1 can (14½ ounces) stewed
   tomatoes
¼ cup small pitted ripe olives
   (optional)
2 teaspoons cornstarch
1½ teaspoons instant chicken
   bouillon granules
8 ounces rotelle noodles, cooked
   Chopped parsley (optional)

• DRAIN pineapple chunks, reserve juice.

• SPRINKLE chicken with garlic powder. In nonstick skillet, brown chicken in oil. Add onion and oregano. Cook until onion is tender.

• ADD tomatoes, pineapple chunks and olives to skillet. Cover; cook 3 more minutes.

• STIR cornstarch and bouillon into reserved juice. Add to skillet. Cook, stirring, until sauce boils and thickens. Cover; cook 5 more minutes.

• SPOON chicken and sauce over noodles. Sprinkle with parsley, if desired.

Makes 4 servings

Broiled Chicken with Honeyed Onion Sauce

Prep and Cook Time: 28 minutes

2 pounds boneless skinless chicken thighs
4 teaspoons olive oil, divided
1 teaspoon paprika
1 teaspoon dried oregano leaves
1 teaspoon salt, divided
½ teaspoon ground cumin
¼ teaspoon black pepper
1 onion, sliced
2 cloves garlic, minced
¼ cup golden raisins
¼ cup honey
2 tablespoons lemon juice

1. Preheat broiler. Rub chicken with 2 teaspoons olive oil. Combine paprika, oregano, ½ teaspoon salt, cumin and pepper; rub mixture over chicken.

2. Place chicken on broiler pan. Broil about 6 inches from heat 5 minutes per side or until chicken is no longer pink in center.

3. While chicken is cooking, heat remaining 2 teaspoons oil in medium nonstick skillet. Add onion and garlic; cook about 8 minutes or until onion is dark golden brown, stirring occasionally.

4. Stir in raisins, honey, lemon juice, remaining ½ teaspoon salt and ¼ cup water. Simmer, uncovered, until slightly thickened. Spoon sauce over chicken. *Makes 4 servings*

Serving Suggestion: Serve with a quick-cooking rice pilaf and mixed green salad.

Chicken Étouffé with Pasta

Prep and Cook Time: 25 minutes

¼ cup vegetable oil
⅓ cup all-purpose flour
½ cup finely chopped onion
4 boneless skinless chicken breast halves (about 1¼ pounds), cut into ¼-inch-thick strips
1 cup chicken broth
1 medium tomato, chopped
¾ cup sliced celery
1 medium green bell pepper, chopped
2 teaspoons Creole or Cajun seasoning blend
Hot cooked pasta

1. Heat oil in large skillet over medium heat until hot. Add flour; cook and stir 10 minutes or until dark brown. Add onion; cook and stir 2 minutes.

2. Stir in chicken, broth, tomato, celery, bell pepper and seasoning blend. Cook 8 minutes or until chicken is no longer pink in center. Serve over pasta. *Makes 6 servings*

Note: Étouffé is a traditional dish from New Orleans. This Cajun stew usually features chicken or shellfish, bell peppers, onions and celery.

Quick Fish & Shellfish

Crispy Tuna Fritters

Prep and Cook Time: 30 minutes

1 cup yellow cornmeal mix
¼ cup minced onion
2 tablespoons minced pimiento
¼ teaspoon salt
⅛ teaspoon ground red pepper
⅛ teaspoon black pepper
¾ cup boiling water
1 can (9 ounces) tuna packed in
　　water, drained
　Vegetable oil
　Cucumber ranch salad dressing
　　or tartar sauce

1. Combine cornmeal mix, onion, pimiento, salt, red pepper and black pepper in small bowl.

2. Slowly stir boiling water into cornmeal mixture. (Mixture will be thick.) Stir in tuna.

3. Pour oil into large skillet to depth of ½ inch; heat over medium heat until hot (about 375°F on deep-fry thermometer).

4. Drop cornmeal mixture by tablespoonfuls into hot oil. Fry over medium heat 1 minute per side or until golden brown. Drain on paper towels. Serve with cucumber ranch salad dressing, if desired. *Makes 6 servings (30 fritters)*

Tuna and Caponata Sauce

Prep Time: 25 minutes

Olive oil
2 cups diced, peeled eggplant
½ cup chopped onion
½ cup chopped celery
½ cup coarsely grated carrot
¼ pound mushrooms, chopped
1 can (14½ ounces) Italian
   pasta-style tomatoes*
1 (7-ounce) pouch of STARKIST
   Flavor Fresh Pouch® Albacore
   or Chunk Light Tuna
Salt and pepper to taste
Hot cooked pasta

*Or substitute 1 can
(14½ ounces) cut-up tomatoes,
½ teaspoon minced or pressed
garlic and 1 teaspoon Italian
herb seasoning.

In 3-quart saucepan, heat several tablespoons olive oil over medium-high heat; sauté ⅓ of eggplant until browned. Remove from pan; set aside. Repeat until all eggplant is browned and reserved. Heat several tablespoons oil; sauté onion, celery, carrot and mushrooms until onion is tender. Return eggplant to saucepan; stir in tomatoes and tuna. Simmer about 15 minutes; add salt and pepper. Serve over pasta.   *Makes 4 servings*

Time-Saving Tip

To prepare the eggplant, rinse under cold running water and pat dry. Trim off the stem end and discard; peel with a vegetable peeler or a paring knife. The flesh of eggplant discolors rapidly, so peel it just before using.

Grilled Snapper with Pesto

Prep and Cook Time: 20 minutes

1½ cups packed fresh basil leaves
1½ cups packed fresh cilantro or
parsley
¼ cup packed fresh mint leaves
¼ cup olive oil
3 tablespoons lime juice
3 cloves garlic, chopped
1 tablespoon sugar
½ teaspoon salt
4 (6-ounce) snapper or grouper
fillets
Black pepper
Lime wedges

1. Combine basil, cilantro, mint, oil, lime juice, garlic, sugar and salt in food processor or blender; process until smooth.

2. Spread about ½ teaspoon pesto on each side of fillets. Sprinkle both sides with pepper to taste. Arrange fish in single layer in grill basket coated with nonstick cooking spray. Grill, covered, over medium-hot coals 3 to 4 minutes per side or until fish flakes easily when tested with fork. Serve with remaining pesto. Garnish with lime wedges if desired. *Makes 4 servings*

Tarragon Scallops & Zucchini

Prep and Cook Time: 20 minutes

1¼ pounds sea scallops
6 tablespoons butter
2 small zucchini, thinly sliced
¼ teaspoon onion powder
2 cups uncooked instant white rice
3 large green onions including
tops, chopped
3 tablespoons chopped fresh
tarragon *or* ¾ teaspoon
dried tarragon leaves
¼ teaspoon salt
2 tablespoons lemon juice
2 teaspoons cornstarch

1. Rinse scallops; pat dry with paper towels. Cut large scallops in half.

2. Melt butter in large nonstick skillet over medium heat. Stir in scallops, zucchini and onion powder; cook and stir 2 minutes. Cover; reduce heat. Cook 7 minutes.

3. Meanwhile, prepare rice according to package directions. Combine green onions, tarragon and salt in small bowl. Blend lemon juice and cornstarch in another small bowl until smooth; set aside.

4. Stir green onion and cornstarch mixtures into skillet. Increase heat to medium; cook and stir 1 minute or until sauce thickens and scallops are opaque. Serve over rice. *Makes 4 servings*

Linguini with Tuna Antipasto

Prep and Cook Time: 18 minutes

1 package (9 ounces) uncooked refrigerated flavored linguini, such as tomato and herb

1 jar (6½ ounces) marinated artichoke hearts, coarsely chopped and liquid reserved

1 can (6 ounces) tuna in water, drained and broken into pieces

½ cup coarsely chopped roasted red peppers

⅓ cup olive oil

¼ cup coarsely chopped black olives

½ teaspoon minced garlic

¼ teaspoon salt

¼ teaspoon red pepper flakes

⅛ teaspoon black pepper

½ cup grated Parmesan cheese

1. Cook linguini according to package directions.

2. Meanwhile, combine remaining ingredients except cheese in large microwavable bowl. Mix well; cover with vented plastic wrap. Microwave at HIGH 2 to 3 minutes or until heated through.

3. Drain linguini; add to bowl. Toss well; arrange on 4 plates. Sprinkle with cheese; garnish as desired. *Makes 4 servings*

Shrimp in Pink Sauce

Prep Time: 5 minutes   **Cook Time:** 15 minutes

1 package (8 ounces) cappellini (angel hair pasta), uncooked

1 package (16 ounces) frozen, cocktail-size shrimp, uncooked

2 cups BIRDS EYE® frozen Broccoli Cuts

1 package (1½ ounces) four cheese sauce mix

¼ cup prepared spaghetti sauce Grated Parmesan cheese

• Cook pasta according to package directions, adding shrimp and broccoli to water 3 minutes before pasta is cooked; drain.

• Cook sauce mix according to package directions. Whisk in spaghetti sauce.

• Toss sauce mixture with pasta, shrimp and broccoli. Serve with Parmesan cheese. *Makes about 4 servings*

Shrimp with Strawberries and Snow Peas

Prep and Cook Time: 20 minutes

1 tablespoon vegetable oil
½ pound peeled medium shrimp
¼ pound snow peas
2 ounces fresh bean sprouts, rinsed
2 cloves garlic, minced
½ teaspoon minced fresh ginger
2 tablespoons brown sugar
2 tablespoons soy sauce
1 tablespoon dark sesame oil
2 teaspoons balsamic vinegar
2 teaspoons oyster sauce
1 cup strawberries, washed, hulled
    and quartered
2 cups hot cooked rice

1. Heat large skillet over medium-high heat until hot. Add vegetable oil. Cook and stir shrimp, snow peas, bean sprouts, garlic and ginger 2 to 3 minutes or until shrimp is opaque and bean sprouts are crisp-tender.

2. Combine brown sugar, soy sauce, sesame oil, vinegar and oyster sauce in small bowl; add to skillet. Cook and stir 1 minute or until brown sugar is dissolved.

3. Remove from heat and stir in strawberries. Serve over rice.

Makes 4 servings

Fish Tacos

Prep Time: 15 minutes   **Total Time:** 30 minutes

1 pound fresh or frozen skinless
    cod, orange roughy or other
    mild fish fillets
2 tablespoons butter or margarine,
    melted
2 teaspoons HERB-OX® chicken
    flavored bouillon granules
¼ teaspoon ground cumin
⅛ teaspoon garlic powder
2 tablespoons mayonnaise or
    salad dressing
2 tablespoons sour cream
1 teaspoon lime juice
1½ cups shredded coleslaw mix
8 (6-inch) flour tortillas, warmed

Heat oven to 450°F. Thaw fish fillets, if frozen. Rinse fish and pat dry with paper towels. Cut fish fillets crosswise into 1-inch slices. Place fish in single layer in a greased shallow pan. Combine butter, bouillon, cumin and garlic powder. Brush over fish. Bake for 4 to 6 minutes or until fish flakes easily when pierced with a fork. Meanwhile, combine mayonnaise, sour cream and lime juice. Add coleslaw mixture; toss to coat. Spoon coleslaw mixture onto each warm tortilla. Top with fish. If desired, serve with salsa.

Makes 6 servings

Tuna in Red Pepper Sauce

Prep and Cook Time: 20 minutes

2 cups chopped red bell peppers
(about 2 peppers)
½ cup chopped onion
1 clove garlic, minced
2 tablespoons vegetable oil
¼ cup dry red or white wine
¼ cup chicken broth
2 teaspoons sugar
¼ teaspoon black pepper
1 red bell pepper, slivered and cut
into ½-inch pieces
1 yellow or green bell pepper,
slivered and cut into
½-inch pieces
½ cup julienne-strip carrots
1 (7-ounce) pouch of STARKIST
Flavor Fresh Pouch® Albacore
or Chunk Light Tuna
Hot cooked pasta or rice

In skillet, sauté chopped bell peppers, onion and garlic in oil for 5 minutes, or until vegetables are very tender. In blender container or food processor bowl, place vegetable mixture; cover and process until puréed. Return to pan; stir in wine, chicken broth, sugar and black pepper. Keep warm. In 2-quart saucepan, steam bell pepper pieces and carrot over simmering water for 5 minutes. Stir steamed vegetables into sauce with tuna; cook for 2 minutes, or until heated through. Serve tuna mixture over pasta. *Makes 4 to 5 servings*

Ricotta Green Chiles and Albacore Sauce

Prep and Cook Time: 15 minutes

1 egg, lightly beaten
1 cup (8 ounces) reduced fat
ricotta cheese
1 cup low fat milk
¼ cup grated Parmesan cheese
2 tablespoons diced green chiles
1 jar (2 ounces) sliced or diced
pimiento, drained
½ teaspoon garlic salt
½ teaspoon ground black pepper
1 (3-ounce) pouch of STARKIST
Flavor Fresh Pouch®
Albacore Tuna
2 cups hot cooked rice

In 1½-quart saucepan, combine all ingredients except tuna and rice; blend well. Heat thoroughly over low heat. Add tuna and rice; heat 1 more minute. *Makes 4 servings*

Note: For a spicier sauce, substitute fresh roasted and chopped Anaheim chiles for the canned mild green chiles.

Oriental Shrimp Burritos

Prep and Cook Time: 10 minutes

1 tablespoon vegetable oil
8 ounces (4 cups packed) shredded cole slaw mix with cabbage and carrots
1 teaspoon bottled minced ginger *or* ½ teaspoon dried ginger
1 teaspoon bottled minced garlic
1 cup bean sprouts
½ cup sliced green onions with tops
8 flour tortillas (6 or 7 inches)
10 to 12 ounces peeled cooked medium shrimp
¼ cup stir-fry sauce
¼ teaspoon red pepper flakes
Plum sauce or sweet-and-sour sauce

1. Heat oil in large, deep skillet over medium-high heat until hot. Add cole slaw mix, ginger and garlic; stir-fry 2 minutes. Add sprouts and onions; stir-fry 3 minutes.

2. While vegetable mixture is cooking, stack tortillas and wrap in wax paper. Microwave at HIGH 1½ minutes or until warm.

3. Add shrimp, stir-fry sauce and red pepper flakes to skillet; stir-fry 2 minutes or until heated through. Spoon about ⅓ cup shrimp mixture evenly down center of each tortilla. Fold 1 end of tortilla over filling and roll up. Serve with plum sauce.

Makes 4 servings

Fish Françoise

Prep Time: 5 minutes   **Cook Time:** 19 minutes

1 can (14½ ounces) DEL MONTE® Diced Tomatoes with Garlic & Onion
1 tablespoon lemon juice
2 cloves garlic, minced
½ teaspoon dried tarragon leaves
⅛ teaspoon black pepper
3 tablespoons whipping cream
Vegetable oil
1½ pounds firm white fish fillets (such as halibut or cod)
Salt
Lemon wedges

1. Preheat broiler; position rack 4 inches from heat.

2. Combine undrained tomatoes, lemon juice, garlic, tarragon and pepper in large saucepan. Cook over medium-high heat about 10 minutes or until liquid has evaporated.

3. Stir in cream. Reduce heat to low. Cook until tomato mixture is very thick; set aside.

4. Brush broiler pan with oil. Arrange fish on pan; season with salt and additional pepper, if desired. Broil 3 to 4 minutes on each side or until fish flakes easily when tested with a fork.

5. Spread tomato mixture over top of fish. Broil 1 minute. Serve with lemon wedges.

Makes 4 servings

Broiled Cajun Fish Fillets

Prep and Cook Time: 20 minutes

2 tablespoons all-purpose flour
½ cup seasoned dried bread crumbs
1 teaspoon dried thyme leaves
½ teaspoon garlic salt
¼ teaspoon ground red pepper
¼ teaspoon black pepper
1 egg
1 tablespoon milk or water
4 orange roughy or scrod fillets,
     ½ inch thick (4 to 5 ounces
     each)
2 tablespoons butter, melted and
     divided
⅓ cup mayonnaise
2 tablespoons sweet pickle relish
1 tablespoon lemon juice
1 teaspoon bottled horseradish

1. Preheat broiler. Place flour in large plastic resealable food storage bag. Combine bread crumbs, thyme, garlic salt, red pepper and black pepper in second bag. Beat together egg and milk; place in third bag.

2. Place each fillet, one at a time, in flour; shake bag to coat lightly. Dip fillets into egg mixture, letting excess drip back into bag. Place fillets, one at a time, in bread crumb mixture; shake to coat well. Transfer fillets to baking sheet coated with nonstick cooking spray.

3. Brush 1 tablespoon butter evenly over fish. Broil 4 to 5 inches from heat 3 minutes. Turn fish; brush with remaining 1 tablespoon butter. Broil 3 minutes or until fish begins to flake when tested with fork.

4. While fish is broiling, combine mayonnaise, relish, juice and horseradish in small bowl; mix well. Serve fish with tartar sauce.

Makes 4 servings

The Tartar Sauce can be prepared in advance. Cover and refrigerate it up to one day before serving. Stir lightly just before serving.

Linguine with Clam Sauce

Prep and Cook Time: 20 minutes

8 ounces uncooked linguine
2 tablespoons olive oil
1 cup chopped onions
1 can (14½ ounces) stewed
    Italian-style tomatoes,
    drained and chopped
2 cloves garlic, crushed
2 teaspoons dried basil leaves
½ cup dry white wine
1 can (10 ounces) whole baby
    clams, drained, juice reserved
⅓ cup chopped fresh parsley
¼ teaspoon *each* salt and black
    pepper

1. Cook linguine according to package directions. Rinse, drain and set aside.

2. While pasta is cooking, heat oil in large skillet over medium heat until hot. Add onions; cook and stir 3 minutes. Add tomatoes, garlic and basil; cook and stir 3 minutes. Stir in wine and reserved clam juice; bring to a boil and simmer, uncovered, 5 minutes.

3. Stir in clams, parsley, salt and pepper. Cook 1 to 2 minutes or until heated through. Spoon over linguine. Serve immediately.

Makes 4 servings

Wild Alaska Salmon, Chickpea and Mint Patties

Prep and Cook Time: 30 minutes

1 can (14.75 ounces) traditional
    pack Alaska salmon, drained
    and chunked
2 cups canned chickpeas, rinsed
    and drained
1 small red onion, chopped
3 garlic cloves, minced
2 teaspoons curry powder
1 medium red chili,* seeded and
    minced
  Fresh mint leaves to taste
1 teaspoon cumin seeds
1 to 2 teaspoons hot pepper sauce
  Salt and black pepper
  All-purpose flour, for dusting
  Olive oil, for frying
1 cup plain low-fat yogurt
2 tablespoons chopped fresh
    cilantro

Place Alaska salmon in blender; add chickpeas, onion, garlic, curry powder, chili, mint, cumin seeds, hot pepper sauce, salt and pepper. Blend together for a few seconds, but do not over blend.

Shape mixture into 18 balls; flatten into patties. Dust lightly with flour.

Heat olive oil in a large frying pan and gently fry patties in batches for about 2 minutes on each side, until golden brown. Drain on paper towels.

Make Coriander Dip by mixing together yogurt and chopped fresh cilantro. Serve with warm patties. *Makes 4 servings*

Favorite recipe from **Alaska Seafood Marketing Institute**

*Chilies can sting and irritate the skin; wear rubber gloves when handling and do not touch eyes. Wash hands after handling.

Linguine with Clam Sauce

Stopwatch Pork

Southwestern Pork Tenderloin

Prep and Cook Time: 20 minutes

2 cups uncooked instant white rice
1 pound pork tenderloin, trimmed
1 teaspoon chili powder
½ teaspoon ground cumin
1 tablespoon olive oil
½ cup frozen chopped green bell pepper
½ cup frozen chopped onion
1 can (10¾ ounces) tomato soup
 Hot pepper sauce
 Black olives, sliced
 Fresh cilantro, chopped

1. Cook rice according to package directions.

2. While rice is cooking, cut pork into ¼-inch-thick slices. Sprinkle both sides of pork slices with chili powder and cumin.

3. Heat oil in large skillet over medium-high heat. Cook pork slices about 3 minutes per side. Remove and set aside.

4. Add bell pepper and onion to skillet; cook and stir 3 minutes. Add soup; bring to a boil. Reduce heat to low. Return pork to skillet and cook 2 minutes or until pork is no longer pink. Add hot pepper sauce to taste. Serve pork slices and sauce over rice. Sprinkle pork with black olives and cilantro, if desired.

Makes 4 servings

Tex-Mex Chops

Prep and Cook Time: 15 minutes

4 boneless pork loin chops, about
    1 pound
1 teaspoon vegetable oil
1½ cups bottled salsa, chunky style
1 can (4 ounces) diced green
    chilies
½ teaspoon ground cumin
¼ cup shredded Cheddar cheese

Heat oil in nonstick pan over medium-high heat. Brown chops on one side, about 2 minutes. Turn chops over. Add salsa, chilies and cumin to skillet; mix well. Lower heat; cover and barely simmer for 8 minutes. Uncover; top each chop with 1 tablespoon cheese. Cover and simmer an additional 2 to 3 minutes or until cheese melts. Serve immediately.

Makes 4 servings

Favorite recipe from **National Pork Board**

Easy Pork Stir-Fry with Peanut Mole

Prep and Cook Time: 15 minutes

1 tablespoon vegetable oil
½ cup chopped onion
1 pound boneless pork chops,
    cut into strips
1¼ teaspoons chili powder
1 teaspoon bottled minced garlic
1 teaspoon ground cumin
¼ teaspoon ground red pepper
1 can (8 ounces) tomato sauce
¼ cup peanut butter
1 tablespoon sugar*
1 tablespoon cornmeal
1 tablespoon unsweetened cocoa
    powder
¼ cup water
8 corn or flour tortillas
    (6 or 7 inches)
1 cup shredded lettuce
1 medium tomato, diced

*For a less sweet sauce, elminate the sugar.

1. Heat oil in large skillet over medium-high heat until hot. Add onion; cook 2 minutes. Add pork, chili powder, garlic, cumin and red pepper. Cook and stir 3 to 4 minutes or until pork is no longer pink in center.

2. Stir in tomato sauce, peanut butter, sugar, cornmeal, cocoa and water. Reduce heat to medium-low; cook 3 to 4 minutes or until smooth and thickened.

3. Distribute pork evenly over tortillas. Top with lettuce and tomatoes; roll up tortillas.

Makes 4 servings

Note: Mole (MOH-lay) is a rich, dark brown Mexican sauce made with ground spices, seeds and nuts, onion, garlic and Mexican chocolate. Many American mole recipes use unsweetened cocoa powder and peanut butter as substitutions for the ground nuts and Mexican chocolate.

Pork and Plum Kabobs

Prep Time: 10 minutes   **Grill Time:** 12 to 14 minutes

¾ pound boneless pork loin chops (1 inch thick), trimmed of fat and cut into 1-inch pieces
1½ teaspoons ground cumin
½ teaspoon ground cinnamon
¼ teaspoon salt
¼ teaspoon garlic powder
¼ teaspoon ground red pepper
¼ cup no-sugar-added red raspberry spread
¼ cup sliced green onions
1 tablespoon orange juice
3 plums, seeded and cut into wedges

1. Place pork in large resealable plastic food storage bag. Combine cumin, cinnamon, salt, garlic powder and red pepper in small bowl. Sprinkle over meat in bag. Shake to coat meat with spices.

2. Prepare grill for direct grilling. Combine raspberry spread, green onions and orange juice in small bowl; set aside.

3. Alternately thread pork and plum wedges onto 8 skewers. Grill kabobs directly over medium heat 12 to 14 minutes or until meat is barely pink in center, turning once during grilling. Brush frequently with reserved raspberry mixture during last 5 minutes of grilling.   *Makes 4 servings*

Pork Chops with Dijon-Dill Sauce

Prep Time: 5 minutes   **Total Time:** 20 minutes

1 pound HORMEL® thin pork loin chops
1 teaspoon oil
2 teaspoons HERB-OX® chicken bouillon granules
¼ teaspoon garlic salt
⅛ teaspoon black pepper
¼ cup plain yogurt
2 teaspoons Dijon mustard
¼ teaspoon dried dill weed
¼ teaspoon sugar

In skillet over medium heat, cook pork chops in oil 6 to 8 minutes, or until cooked through and pork reaches an internal temperature of 155°F. Remove pork to platter; season with bouillon, garlic salt and black pepper. In small bowl, combine yogurt, mustard, dill weed and sugar. Serve sauce with pork chops.   *Makes 4 servings*

Pork Tenderloin with Apple-Raisin Sauce

Prep and Cook Time: 20 minutes

4 tablespoons butter, divided
1½ pounds pork tenderloin cutlets
½ cup chicken broth
1 tablespoon cornstarch
1 cup chopped onion
1 teaspoon minced garlic
½ teaspoon dried rosemary
1 cup prepared chunky applesauce
½ cup white wine Worcestershire
    sauce
⅓ cup raisins
½ cup whipping cream

1. Melt 2 tablespoons butter in heavy large skillet over medium heat. Add pork and cook about 2½ minutes per side or until no longer pink in center. Transfer pork to serving plate. Cover and keep warm.

2. Combine broth and cornstarch in small bowl; stir until smooth. Set aside.

3. Melt remaining 2 tablespoons butter in same skillet over medium heat. Add onion, garlic and rosemary; cook and stir 2 minutes. Add applesauce, white wine Worcestershire sauce, raisins and broth mixture; bring to a boil. Gradually stir in whipping cream. Return to a boil.

4. Pour sauce over pork slices and serve immediately.

Makes 6 servings

Pork Pitas with Fruity Mustard Salsa

Prep Time: 15 minutes   **Cook Time:** 10 minutes

1 pound boneless pork chops or
    chicken breast halves
4 tablespoons **French's®** Classic
    Yellow® Mustard, divided
1 cup chopped canned peaches,
    drained
⅓ cup finely chopped red bell
    pepper
1 small green onion, minced
1 tablespoon minced cilantro leaves
1 teaspoon **Frank's® RedHot®**
    Original Cayenne Pepper
    Sauce
6 large soft pita breads or pita
    pocket bread, heated

Preheat broiler or grill. Brush chops with *2 tablespoons* mustard. Broil or grill 10 to 15 minutes or until no longer pink in center. Set aside.

Combine peaches, bell pepper, onion, remaining *2 tablespoons mustard,* cilantro and **Frank's RedHot** Sauce in medium bowl.

To serve, thinly slice chops. Arrange pork in center of pitas. Spoon salsa on top. Fold in half to serve.   *Makes 6 servings*

Pork Spiedini

Prep Time: 15 minutes   **Cook Time:** 10 minutes

2 pounds boneless pork loin, cut into 1-inch cubes
¾ cup cider vinegar
¾ cup olive oil
¼ cup lemon juice
1 tablespoon Worcestershire sauce
1 tablespoon dried oregano
2 cloves garlic, minced
2 teaspoons ground black pepper
1 teaspoon salt
1 teaspoon dried thyme
½ teaspoon cayenne pepper
6 thick slices Italian bread

Combine all ingredients, except bread, in resealable plastic food storage bag; refrigerate 4 to 24 hours. Remove pork cubes from marinade; thread pork onto skewers. (If using bamboo skewers, soak in water for 1 hour to prevent burning.) Grill over hot coals, basting with reserved marinade, for 4 to 5 minutes; discard marinade. Turn kabobs and grill 4 minutes. Serve by pulling meat off of skewer onto Italian bread.

Makes 6 servings

Favorite recipe from **National Pork Board**

Louisiana Pork Chops

Prep Time: 5 minutes   **Cook Time:** 21 minutes

1 teaspoon garlic powder
¼ teaspoon black pepper
¼ teaspoon white pepper
¼ teaspoon cayenne pepper
4 pork chops, ¾ inch thick
1 tablespoon butter or margarine
1 can (14½ ounces) DEL MONTE® Diced Tomatoes with Green Pepper & Onion

1. Combine garlic powder and peppers. Sprinkle on both sides of meat.

2. Heat butter in large skillet over medium-high heat. Add meat; cook 5 minutes. Turn over and cook 4 minutes; drain. Add tomatoes.

3. Cover and cook over medium heat 10 minutes or until meat is cooked. Remove meat to serving dish; keep warm. Cook sauce until thickened; spoon over meat. *Makes 4 servings*

Fried Rice with Ham

Prep and Cook Time: 18 minutes

2 tablespoons vegetable oil, divided
2 eggs, beaten
1 small onion, chopped
1 carrot, peeled and chopped
⅔ cup diced ham
½ cup frozen green peas
1 large clove garlic, minced
3 cups cold cooked rice
3 tablespoons reduced-sodium soy
    sauce
⅛ teaspoon black pepper

1. Heat 1 tablespoon oil in large skillet or wok over medium-high heat until hot. Add eggs; rotate skillet to swirl eggs into thin layer. Cook eggs until set and slightly brown; break up with wooden spoon. Remove from skillet to small bowl.

2. Heat remaining 1 tablespoon oil until hot. Add onion and carrot; stir-fry 2 minutes. Add ham, peas and garlic; stir-fry 1 minute.

3. Add rice; stir-fry 2 to 3 minutes or until rice is heated through. Stir in soy sauce and pepper until well blended. Stir in cooked eggs.

Makes 4 servings

Time-Saving Tip

Substitute ¾ cup of frozen carrot and pea mixture for the fresh carrot and green peas called for in the recipe.

Speedy Pork Cassoulet

Prep and Cook Time: 30 minutes

3 boneless pork chops, cut into
 ¾-inch cubes
1 tablespoon vegetable oil
2 medium onions, chopped
2 cloves garlic, minced
2 cans (15 ounces each) cannellini
 or Great Northern beans,
 rinsed and drained
¾ cup chicken broth
⅓ cup chopped sun-dried tomatoes
 packed in oil, drained
1 teaspoon dried rosemary, crushed
1 teaspoon dried thyme, crushed
¼ teaspoon salt
¼ teaspoon pepper
¼ cup chopped fresh parsley
¼ cup seasoned bread crumbs

In Dutch oven heat oil over medium-high heat. Cook and stir onions and garlic until tender but not brown. Add pork; cook and stir 2 to 3 minutes or until browned. Stir in beans, chicken broth, sun-dried tomatoes and seasonings except parsley. Bring to boiling; reduce heat, cover and simmer 10 minutes or just until pork is tender, stirring occasionally. Spoon cassoulet into individual soup bowls. Sprinkle each serving with parsley and bread crumbs.

Makes 4 servings

Favorite recipe from **National Pork Board**

Pork Chops with Balsamic Vinegar

Prep and Cook Time: 20 minutes

2 boneless center pork loin chops,
 1½ inch thick
1½ teaspoons lemon pepper
1 teaspoon vegetable oil
3 tablespoons balsamic vinegar
2 tablespoons chicken broth
2 teaspoons butter

Pat chops dry. Coat with lemon pepper. Heat oil in heavy skillet over medium-high heat. Add chops. Brown on first side 8 minutes; turn and cook 7 minutes more or until done. Remove from pan and keep warm. Add vinegar and broth to skillet; cook, stirring, until syrupy (about 1 to 2 minutes). Stir in butter until blended. Spoon sauce over chops.

Makes 2 servings

Favorite recipe from **National Pork Board**

Pork Tenderloin with Mandarin Salsa

Prep and Cook Time: 21 minutes

1½ pounds boneless pork loin chops, cut into ¼-inch strips

1 cup orange juice

1 medium green bell pepper, finely chopped

1 can (10½ ounces) mandarin orange segments, drained and chopped

1⅓ cups red onion, chopped, divided

½ cup frozen whole kernel corn, thawed

2 tablespoons olive oil, divided

4 teaspoons bottled minced garlic, divided

1½ teaspoons chili powder, divided

1¼ teaspoons salt, divided

1½ teaspoons cumin

¼ teaspoon black pepper

1. Combine pork and orange juice in medium bowl. Set aside.

2. In another medium bowl, combine bell pepper, mandarin segments, ⅓ cup onion, corn, 1 tablespoon oil, 1 teaspoon garlic, ¼ teaspoon chili powder and ¼ teaspoon salt. Set aside.

3. Heat remaining 1 tablespoon oil in large nonstick skillet over medium-high heat. Add remaining 1 cup onion and 3 teaspoons garlic. Cook and stir 5 minutes or until softened and starting to brown.

4. While onion and garlic are cooking, drain pork, reserving orange juice. Toss pork, remaining 1¼ teaspoons chili powder, remaining 1 teaspoon salt, cumin and black pepper. Add pork to skillet; cook and stir 5 minutes or until pork is cooked through and lightly browned. Add ⅓ cup reserved orange juice marinade to skillet. Bring mixture to a boil. Reduce heat to medium; simmer 1 to 2 minutes or until liquid thickens slightly. Serve immediately with mandarin salsa.

Makes 4 servings

Stir-Fried Pork Burritos

Prep and Cook Time: 20 minutes

1 pound lean boneless pork loin
2 cloves garlic, minced
1 teaspoon dried oregano, crushed
1 teaspoon ground cumin
1 teaspoon seasoned salt
2 tablespoons orange juice
2 tablespoons vinegar
½ teaspoon hot pepper sauce,
   or to taste
1 tablespoon vegetable oil
1 medium onion, peeled and sliced
1 sweet green bell pepper, seeded
   and sliced
4 flour tortillas

Slice pork across grain into ⅛-inch strips. Mix together garlic, oregano, cumin, salt, orange juice, vinegar and hot pepper sauce. Marinate pork strips in mixture for 10 minutes. Heat oil in heavy skillet or on griddle until hot. Stir-fry pork strips, onion, and bell pepper until pork is no longer pink, about 3 to 5 minutes. Serve with flour tortillas, sliced green onion, shredded lettuce and salsa, if desired.   *Makes 4 servings*

Favorite recipe from **National Pork Board**

Hearty Italian Medley

Prep Time: 10 minutes   **Cook Time:** 17 minutes

1 pound hot Italian sausage, cut
   into bite-size pieces
1 onion, chopped
3 zucchini, chunked
1 eggplant, chunked
1 DOLE® Green Bell Pepper,
   seeded, chunked
¼ cup water
2 cups prepared marinara sauce
3 cups DOLE® Fresh Pineapple,
   cut into chunks
1 tomato, chunked
4 cups hot cooked noodles

• Brown sausage and onion in large skillet or Dutch oven. Add zucchini, eggplant, bell pepper and water. Cover; simmer 10 minutes until tender.

• Stir in marinara sauce, pineapple chunks and tomato. Simmer 5 minutes. Serve over hot cooked noodles.   *Makes 8 servings*

Clock"wise" Beef

Tamale Pie

Prep and Cook Time: 20 minutes

1 pound ground beef
1 package (10 ounces) frozen
    corn, thawed
1 can (14½ ounces) diced
    tomatoes, undrained
1 can (4 ounces) sliced black
    olives, drained
1 package (1¼ ounces) taco
    seasoning mix
1 package (6 ounces) corn muffin
    or corn bread mix plus
    ingredients to prepare mix
¼ cup (1 ounce) shredded Cheddar
    cheese
1 green onion, thinly sliced
    Papaya, cut into wedges
    (optional)
    Lime juice (optional)

1. Preheat oven to 400°F. Place meat in large skillet; cook over high heat 6 to 8 minutes or until meat is no longer pink, stirring to separate meat. Pour off drippings. Add corn, tomatoes, olives and seasoning mix to meat. Bring to a boil over medium-high heat, stirring constantly. Pour into deep 9-inch pie plate; smooth top with spatula.

2. Prepare corn muffin mix according to package directions. Spread evenly over meat mixture. Bake 8 to 10 minutes or until golden brown. Sprinkle with cheese and onion. Let stand 10 minutes before serving. Serve with papaya sprinkled with lime juice, if desired.　　　　　*Makes 6 servings*

Zesty Mexican Stir-Fry Fajitas

Prep Time: 10 minutes   **Cook Time:** 10 minutes

1 pound beef sirloin, flank or round steak, thinly sliced
1 large red bell pepper, thinly sliced
1 medium onion, sliced
1 jar (12 ounces) prepared beef gravy
2 tablespoons **Frank's® RedHot®** Original Cayenne Pepper Sauce
1 teaspoon garlic powder
1 teaspoon dried oregano leaves
1 teaspoon ground cumin
8 flour tortillas, heated

1. Heat *2 tablespoons oil* in large skillet over high heat until hot. Stir-fry beef in batches 5 minutes or until browned.

2. Add pepper and onion; cook 2 minutes. Add remaining ingredients except tortillas. Stir-fry an additional 2 minutes. Spoon mixture into tortillas; roll up. Splash on more **Frank's RedHot** Sauce to taste.
Makes 4 servings

Burgundy Beef Pasta

Prep Time: 10 minutes   **Cook Time:** 20 minutes

8 ounces uncooked linguine
1 pound top sirloin, very thinly sliced crosswise
2 cloves garlic, minced
½ teaspoon dried thyme leaves
2 teaspoons vegetable oil
¼ pound fresh mushrooms, sliced
1 can (14½ ounces) DEL MONTE® Stewed Tomatoes, No Salt Added with Onions, Celery & Green Peppers
1 can (8 ounces) DEL MONTE Tomato Sauce (No Salt Added)
¾ cup dry red wine
Chopped parsley (optional)

1. Cook pasta according to package directions; drain.

2. Cook sirloin, garlic and thyme in oil in large skillet over medium-high heat 3 minutes.

3. Add mushrooms; cook 1 minute. Add undrained tomatoes, tomato sauce and wine.

4. Cook, uncovered, over medium heat 15 minutes, stirring occasionally. Serve over pasta. Garnish with chopped parsley, if desired.
Makes 4 servings

Cook pasta ahead; rinse and drain. Cover and refrigerate. Just before serving, heat in microwave or dip in boiling water.

Beef & Salsa Salad Supreme

Prep and Cook Time: 20 minutes

1 boneless beef top sirloin steak (about 1 pound)
2 teaspoons Mexican seasoning blend or chili powder
1 package (8 ounces) assorted torn salad greens
1 cup rinsed, drained canned black beans
1 cup frozen corn, thawed
¼ cup picante sauce or salsa
¼ cup red wine vinegar and oil salad dressing
1 medium tomato, chopped
4 sprigs cilantro

1. Heat large nonstick skillet over medium heat. Rub both sides of steak with seasoning. Cook steak in skillet 5 minutes per side to medium-rare or until desired doneness. Transfer steak to cutting board; tent with foil. Let stand 5 minutes.

2. While steak is cooking, combine salad greens, beans and corn in large bowl. Combine picante sauce and dressing in small bowl; add to greens mixture. Toss lightly to coat. Arrange on salad plates.

3. Carve steak crosswise into ¼-inch strips; arrange over salad greens, dividing evenly. Sprinkle with chopped tomato and cilantro.

Makes 4 servings

Cheesy Taco Pasta Shells

Prep Time: 10 minutes   **Cook Time:** 20 minutes

2 tablespoons margarine or butter
1 (6.2-ounce) package PASTA RONI® Shells & White Cheddar
⅔ cup milk
2 cups cooked steak or ground beef or chicken strips
1½ cups chopped tomatoes
¼ cup sliced green onions or yellow onion
1 package taco seasoning mix
Salsa

1. In medium saucepan, bring 2¾ cups water and margarine to a boil. Reduce heat to medium. Add pasta; boil, uncovered, 12 minutes or until most of water is absorbed, stirring frequently.

2. Stir in milk, steak, tomatoes, green onions, taco seasoning mix and Special Seasonings. Cook 4 minutes or until pasta is tender. Serve topped with salsa.

Makes 4 servings

Beef Stroganoff and Zucchini Topped Potatoes

Prep and Cook Time: 25 minutes

4 baking potatoes (8 ounces each)
¾ pound ground beef
¾ cup chopped onion
1 cup sliced mushrooms
2 tablespoons ketchup
1 beef bouillon cube
1 teaspoon Worcestershire sauce
¼ teaspoon black pepper
¼ teaspoon hot pepper sauce
1 medium zucchini, cut into
    matchstick-size strips
½ cup sour cream, divided

1. Pierce potatoes in several places with fork. Place in microwave oven on paper towel. Microwave potatoes at HIGH 15 minutes or until softened. Wrap in paper towels. Let stand 5 minutes.

2. While potatoes are cooking, heat large nonstick skillet over medium-high heat until hot. Add beef and onion. Cook and stir 5 minutes or until beef is browned. Add all remaining ingredients except zucchini and sour cream. Cover; simmer 5 minutes. Add zucchini. Cover and cook 3 minutes. Remove from heat. Stir in ¼ cup sour cream. Cover; let stand 5 minutes.

3. Cut open potatoes. Divide beef mixture evenly among potatoes. Top with remaining ¼ cup sour cream.

Makes 4 servings

Steak Diane with Couscous

Prep and Cook Time: 18 minutes

1 can (14½ ounces) beef broth,
    divided
1 cup frozen peas
1 cup uncooked couscous
2 tablespoons butter, divided
4 boneless beef tenderloin
    or top loin (strip) steaks
    (5 to 6 ounces each)
¼ teaspoon black pepper
8 ounces sliced button or wild
    mushrooms, such as
    portobello or shiitake
½ cup chopped onion
1 tablespoon Dijon mustard
1 tablespoon Worcestershire sauce

1. Reserve ¼ cup broth. Bring remaining broth and peas to a boil in medium saucepan over high heat. Stir in couscous; cover and remove from heat. Let stand while preparing steaks.

2. Melt 1 tablespoon butter in medium skillet over medium-high heat. Sprinkle both sides of steaks with pepper; add to skillet. Cook 3 to 4 minutes per side for medium-rare or to desired doneness. Transfer to plate; set aside.

3. Melt remaining 1 tablespoon butter in same skillet; add mushrooms and onion. Cook 2 minutes, stirring occasionally. Stir in reserved ¼ cup broth, mustard and Worcestershire sauce. Simmer 2 minutes or until sauce thickens. Return steaks to skillet; heat through, turning steaks and stirring mushrooms once.

4. Spoon couscous mixture onto 4 serving plates. Top with steaks and sauce.

Makes 4 servings

Note: Tender filet mignon or strip steaks are a good choice for this recipe.

Steak Stir-Fry

Prep and Cook Time: 20 minutes

1 beef top sirloin steak
(about 1½ pounds)
1 package (8 ounces) dry rice
stick noodles
¼ cup dry white wine
¼ cup soy sauce
1 tablespoon plus 1½ teaspoons
cornstarch
1 tablespoon sugar
2 teaspoons minced fresh ginger
2 tablespoons vegetable oil
2 teaspoons minced garlic
2 cups sliced mushrooms
2 cups matchstick-size carrot sticks
1 cup green bell pepper strips
½ cup sliced green onions
4 cups fresh spinach leaves

1. Cut beef lengthwise in half, then crosswise into ¼-inch strips. Set aside. Cook noodles according to package directions. Drain well. Set aside.

2. While noodles are cooking, combine wine, soy sauce, cornstarch, sugar and ginger in medium bowl; whisk to blend. Add beef strips; toss to coat well. Set aside.

3. Heat oil and garlic in large nonstick skillet or wok over high heat. Add mushrooms, carrots, bell peppers and green onions; stir-fry 4 minutes. Transfer vegetables to bowl. Cover; keep warm.

4. Add beef strips and marinade to skillet; stir-fry 6 minutes. Return vegetables to skillet; stir until blended.

5. Line serving platter with spinach. Arrange noodles over spinach; top with beef mixture.   *Makes 4 servings*

Tip: Stir-fry meat can be purchased presliced from the supermarket meat case.

Bistro Steak with Mushrooms

Prep Time: 10 minutes   **Cook Time:** 20 minutes

1½ to 2 pounds boneless sirloin
steak (1½ inches thick)
2 cups sliced mushrooms
1 can (10¾ ounces) condensed
golden mushroom soup
½ cup dry red wine or beef broth
3 tablespoons **French's**®
Worcestershire Sauce

1. Rub sides of steak with ¼ *teaspoon pepper*. Heat *1 tablespoon oil* over medium-high heat in nonstick skillet. Cook steak about 5 minutes per side for medium-rare or to desired doneness. Transfer steak to platter.

2. Stir-fry mushrooms in same skillet in *1 tablespoon oil* until browned. Stir in soup, wine, Worcestershire and ¼ *cup water*. Bring to a boil. Simmer, stirring, 3 minutes. Return steak and juices to skillet. Cook until heated through. Serve with mashed potatoes, if desired.   *Makes 6 servings*

Mediterranean Meatballs and Couscous

Prep and Cook Time: 25 minutes

2½ cups water
1 can (14½ ounces) chicken broth
1½ cups precooked couscous*
¾ cup golden raisins
¼ cup chopped fresh parsley
3 tablespoons lemon juice, divided
3 teaspoons grated lemon peel, divided
2 teaspoons ground cinnamon, divided
1 teaspoon turmeric
½ teaspoon ground cumin
1 pound ground beef
½ cup crushed saltine crackers
¼ cup evaporated skimmed milk
½ teaspoon dried oregano leaves
Lemon wedges (optional)
Fresh oregano (optional)

Check package ingredient list for "precooked semolina."

1. Pour water and broth into 2-quart saucepan. Bring to a boil over high heat. Remove from heat. Add couscous, raisins, parsley, 2 tablespoons lemon juice, 2 teaspoons lemon peel, 1½ teaspoons cinnamon, turmeric and cumin. Cover; let stand 5 minutes.

2. Combine beef, crackers, milk, remaining 1 tablespoon lemon juice, 1 teaspoon lemon peel, ½ teaspoon cinnamon and oregano in large bowl. Mix until well blended. Shape into 24 balls. Place in large microwavable baking dish. Cover loosely with waxed paper. Microwave at HIGH 4 minutes or until meatballs are cooked through.

3. Stir couscous mixture and spoon onto serving platter. Arrange meatballs on couscous. Garnish with lemon wedges and fresh oregano, if desired. *Makes 6 servings*

Pasta Picadillo

Prep Time: 10 minutes   **Cook Time:** 20 minutes

12 ounces uncooked medium shell pasta
Nonstick cooking spray
1 pound 95% lean ground beef
⅔ cup finely chopped green bell pepper
½ cup finely chopped onion
2 cloves garlic, minced
1 (8-ounce) can tomato sauce
½ cup water
⅓ cup raisins
3 tablespoons chopped pimiento-stuffed green olives
2 tablespoons drained capers
2 tablespoons vinegar
½ teaspoon black pepper
¼ teaspoon salt

1. Cook pasta according to package directions, omitting salt. Drain; set aside.

2. While pasta is cooking, spray large nonstick skillet with cooking spray. Add beef, bell pepper, onion and garlic. Brown beef over medium-high heat 5 minutes or until no longer pink, stirring to separate meat; drain fat. Stir in remaining ingredients. Reduce heat to medium-low; cook, covered, 15 minutes, stirring occasionally.

3. Add cooked pasta to skillet; toss to coat. Cover and heat through, about 2 minutes. *Makes 6 (1-cup) servings*

Curry Beef

Prep and Cook Time: 30 minutes

12 ounces wide egg noodles *or*
    1⅓ cups long-grain white rice
1 tablespoon olive oil
1 medium onion, thinly sliced
1 tablespoon curry powder
1 teaspoon ground cumin
2 cloves garlic, minced
1 pound 95% lean ground beef
1 cup (8 ounces) sour cream
½ cup 2% milk
½ cup raisins, divided
1 teaspoon sugar
¼ cup chopped walnuts, almonds
    or pecans

1. Cook noodles according to package directions.

2. Meanwhile, heat oil in large skillet over medium-high heat until hot. Add onion; cook and stir 3 to 4 minutes. Add curry powder, cumin and garlic; cook 2 to 3 minutes longer or until onion is tender. Add meat; cook 6 to 8 minutes or until meat is no longer pink, stirring to separate meat.

3. Stir in sour cream, milk, ¼ cup raisins and sugar. Reduce heat to medium; cook, stirring constantly, until heated through. Spoon over drained noodles. Sprinkle with remaining ¼ cup raisins and nuts.

Makes 4 servings

Tomato Ginger Beef

Prep Time: 10 minutes   **Cook Time:** 12 minutes

2 tablespoons dry sherry
1 tablespoon soy sauce
2 cloves garlic, crushed
1 teaspoon minced gingerroot *or*
    ¼ teaspoon ground ginger
1 pound flank steak, thinly sliced
1 tablespoon cornstarch
1 tablespoon vegetable oil
1 can (14½ ounces) DEL MONTE®
    Diced Tomatoes with Garlic
    & Onion
Hot cooked rice

1. Combine sherry, soy sauce, garlic and ginger; toss with meat. Stir in cornstarch; mix well.

2. Cook meat mixture in oil in large skillet over high heat until browned, stirring constantly.

3. Add tomatoes; cook over high heat until thickened, stirring frequently, about 5 minutes. Serve over hot cooked rice. Garnish with sliced green onions, if desired.

Makes 4 to 6 servings

Meat and Potato Stir-Fry

Prep and Cook Time: 25 minutes

1 tablespoon vegetable oil
1 large baking potato, peeled and
    cut into ½-inch cubes
2 medium carrots, peeled and
    thinly sliced
1 medium onion, halved and sliced
⅔ cup beef broth
1 teaspoon salt, divided
1 pound 90% lean ground beef
1 large clove garlic, minced
1 tablespoon dried parsley flakes
1 teaspoon paprika
½ teaspoon ground cinnamon
½ teaspoon ground cumin
¼ teaspoon black pepper
    Pita bread (optional)

1. Heat oil in large skillet or wok over medium-high heat until hot. Add potato, carrots and onion; cook and stir 3 minutes. Stir in broth and ½ teaspoon salt. Reduce heat to medium. Cover and cook 6 to 7 minutes or until potato is tender, stirring once or twice. Remove vegetables from skillet; set aside. Wipe out skillet with paper towel.

2. Heat skillet over medium-high heat until hot. Add ground beef and garlic; stir-fry 3 minutes or until meat is no longer pink. Add parsley, paprika, cinnamon, cumin, remaining ½ teaspoon salt and pepper; cook and stir 1 minute. Add vegetables; heat through. Serve as filling for pita bread, if desired.

Makes 4 servings

Skewered Beef Strips with Spicy Honey Glaze

Prep and Cook Time: 30 minutes

1 beef top sirloin steak
    (about 1 pound)
⅓ cup soy sauce
2 tablespoons white vinegar
1 teaspoon ground ginger
⅛ teaspoon ground red pepper
⅓ cup honey

1. Slice beef across the grain into ¼-inch-thick strips. Thread beef strips onto 12 skewers* and place in large glass baking dish.

2. Heat broiler or prepare grill. Combine soy sauce, vinegar, ginger and red pepper; pour over skewers and marinate 10 minutes, turning once.

3. Drain marinade into small saucepan; stir in honey and brush mixture over beef. Bring remaining mixture to a boil; boil 2 minutes.

4. Broil or grill skewered beef 3 to 4 minutes. Serve remaining honey glaze as dipping sauce. *Makes 4 servings*

Soak wooden skewers in cold water 20 minutes before using to prevent them from burning.

Timely Vegetarian

Sweet & Sour Vegetable Couscous

Prep and Cook Time: 20 minutes

1 can (14½ ounces) vegetable broth
1 box (10 ounces) uncooked couscous
1 tablespoon vegetable oil
3 cups frozen Asian blend vegetable mix
⅓ cup stir-fry sauce
2 tablespoons honey
2 tablespoons lemon juice
¼ cup sliced almonds

1. Pour vegetable broth into medium saucepan; bring to a boil. Stir in couscous and oil. Remove from heat; cover and let stand 5 minutes or until liquid is absorbed. Fluff couscous with fork; cover to keep warm.

2. Meanwhile, place vegetables in microwavable dish. Microwave according to package directions; drain.

3. Combine stir-fry sauce, honey and lemon juice in small bowl. Pour over cooked vegetables; microwave at HIGH 1 minute.

4. Spoon couscous onto serving plates. Top with vegetable mixture and sprinkle with almonds. *Makes 4 servings*

Note: For extra flavor and crunch, toast almonds. Place in small nonstick skillet; cook and stir over medium heat 2 minutes or until golden brown. (Watch carefully to prevent burning.)

Grilled Portobello & Pepper Wraps

Prep and Cook Time: 18 minutes

1 container (8 ounces) sour cream
1 teaspoon dried dill weed
1 teaspoon onion powder
2 tablespoons vegetable oil
1 large clove garlic, minced
2 portobello mushrooms, stems
    removed
1 large green bell pepper,
    quartered
1 large red bell pepper, quartered
    Salt and black pepper to taste
6 (6-inch) flour tortillas, warmed
    Spicy refried beans (optional)

1. Prepare grill for direct cooking. Combine sour cream, dill weed and onion powder in small bowl; set aside. Combine oil and garlic in small bowl; set aside.

2. Spray grid with nonstick cooking spray. Place mushrooms and bell peppers on prepared grid. Brush lightly with oil mixture; season with salt and black pepper.

3. Grill over medium-hot coals 10 minutes or until peppers are crisp-tender, turning halfway through grilling time. Remove mushrooms and peppers to cutting board; cut into 1-inch slices.

4. Place on serving platter. Serve with sour cream mixture, tortillas and refried beans, if desired.

Makes 4 to 6 servings

Sun-Dried Tomato Pesto with Tortellini

Prep and Cook Time: 20 minutes

2 packages (9 ounces each)
    refrigerated three-cheese
    tortellini
¼ cup slivered almonds or walnuts
10 oil-packed sun-dried tomatoes
3 cloves garlic
½ cup fresh parsley leaves,
    coarsely chopped
¼ cup fresh basil leaves, coarsely
    chopped
¼ cup grated Parmesan cheese
2 teaspoons olive oil
    Fresh basil

1. Cook pasta according to package directions.

2. Meanwhile, toast almonds in heavy skillet over low heat 3 to 4 minutes or until lightly browned, stirring frequently. Remove almonds from skillet; cool.

3. Combine tomatoes, garlic, parsley, almonds, ¼ cup basil, Parmesan and oil in food processor or blender; process until well blended. (If pesto is too dry, add hot pasta cooking water, 1 teaspoon at a time, until desired consistency.)

4. Combine tortellini and pesto in serving bowl; toss to combine. Garnish with additional fresh basil, if desired.

Makes 6 servings

Savory Bean Stew

Prep and Cook Time: 30 minutes

1 tablespoon olive or vegetable oil
1 cup frozen vegetable blend
    (onions, celery, red and
    green bell peppers)
1 can (15½ ounces) chick-peas
    (garbanzo beans), rinsed and
    drained
1 can (15 ounces) pinto beans,
    rinsed and drained
1 can (15 ounces) black beans,
    rinsed and drained
1 can (14½ ounces) diced tomatoes
    with roasted garlic, undrained
¾ teaspoon dried thyme leaves
¾ teaspoon dried sage leaves
½ to ¾ teaspoon dried oregano
    leaves
¾ cup vegetable broth, divided
1 tablespoon all-purpose flour
    Salt and black pepper to taste

Polenta
3 cups water
¾ cup yellow cornmeal
¾ teaspoon salt
    Black pepper to taste

1. Heat oil in large saucepan over medium heat until hot. Add vegetable blend; cook and stir 5 minutes. Stir in beans, tomatoes with juice and herbs. Mix ½ cup vegetable broth and flour. Stir into bean mixture; bring to a boil. Boil, stirring constantly, 1 minute. Reduce heat to low; simmer, covered, 10 minutes. Add remaining ¼ cup broth; season with salt and black pepper.

2. While stew is simmering, prepare Polenta. Bring 3 cups water to a boil. Reduce heat to medium; gradually stir in cornmeal and salt. Cook 5 to 8 minutes or until cornmeal thickens and holds its shape, but is still soft. Season with black pepper. Spread Polenta over plate and top with stew.

Makes 6 (1-cup) servings

Tortellini with Artichokes, Olives and Feta Cheese

Prep and Cook Time: 23 minutes

2 packages (9 ounces) refrigerated cheese-filled spinach tortellini

2 jars (4 ounces) marinated artichoke heart quarters, drained*

½ cup sliced pitted ripe olives

2 medium carrots, diagonally sliced

½ cup (2 ounces) crumbled feta cheese

½ cup cheese-garlic Italian salad dressing

Black pepper to taste

For additional flavor, add some artichoke marinade to tortellini with salad dressing.

1. Cook pasta according to package directions. Remove and rinse well under cold water until pasta is cool.

2. Combine pasta, artichoke hearts, olives, carrots and feta cheese in large bowl. Add salad dressing; toss lightly. Season with black pepper.

Makes 6 servings

Serving Suggestion: Serve with whole-wheat dinner rolls and fresh melons such as honeydew, watermelon, cantaloupe or Crenshaw.

Chick-Pea Patties

Prep and Cook Time: 18 minutes

1 can (15 ounces) chick-peas (garbanzo beans), rinsed and drained

1 cup shredded carrots

⅓ cup seasoned dry bread crumbs

2 tablespoons creamy Italian salad dressing

1 egg

2 tablespoons vegetable oil

1. Mash chick-peas coarsely in medium bowl with hand potato masher, leaving some larger pieces. Stir in carrots, bread crumbs, dressing and egg.

2. Shape chick-pea mixture into 4 patties.

3. Heat oil in large nonstick skillet over medium-high heat. Add patties; cook 3 minutes per side or until well browned.

4. Remove from skillet; drain on paper towels. Serve immediately.

Makes 4 servings

Grilled Fruits with Orange Couscous

Prep and Cook Time: 28 minutes

1⅓ cups quick-cooking couscous
½ teaspoon ground cinnamon
½ cup orange juice
2 tablespoons vegetable oil, divided
1 tablespoon soy sauce
1 tablespoon maple syrup
⅛ teaspoon ground nutmeg
½ cup raisins
½ cup chopped walnuts or pecans
2 ripe mangoes, quartered
½ fresh pineapple, cut into
    ½-inch slices

1. Prepare grill for direct cooking.

2. Prepare couscous according to package directions, adding cinnamon to water with couscous.

3. Meanwhile, blend orange juice, 1 tablespoon oil, soy sauce and maple syrup in glass measuring cup; set aside. Blend remaining 1 tablespoon oil and nutmeg in small bowl; set aside.

4. Cool couscous 5 minutes. Stir in orange juice mixture, raisins and walnuts. Transfer to serving bowl. Place bowl in center of large serving platter. Cover lightly.

5. Spray grid with nonstick cooking spray. Place mangoes, skin side down, and pineapple on prepared grid. Brush fruits with nutmeg mixture.

6. Grill over medium-hot coals 5 to 7 minutes or until fruits soften, turning pineapple halfway through grilling time. Arrange grilled fruits around couscous on platter. *Makes 4 servings*

Time-Saving Tip

Purchase pineapple already trimmed and cored in refrigerated produce section. Or, try cantaloupe wedges instead of mango.

Broccoli and Carrot Linguine

Prep and Cook Time: 20 minutes

1 package (9 ounces) refrigerated linguine, cut in half
1 tablespoon olive oil
1 cup shredded carrots
¼ cup Italian salad dressing
1 tablespoon red wine vinegar
1 teaspoon sugar
½ teaspoon black pepper
1 cup petite frozen broccoli florets, cooked and drained
1 cup grated Parmesan cheese

1. Cook pasta according to package directions. Drain well.

2. While pasta is cooking, heat oil in large nonstick skillet over medium heat until hot. Add carrots, salad dressing, vinegar, sugar and pepper; cook and stir 2 minutes. Remove from heat.

3. Combine pasta, broccoli and carrot mixture in large serving bowl. Add cheese; toss to combine. *Makes 6 servings*

Cheese Tortellini in Tomato Cream Sauce

Prep Time: 5 minutes   **Cook Time:** 20 minutes

1 jar (1 pound 10 ounces) RAGÚ® Chunky Gardenstyle Pasta Sauce
⅔ cup whipping or heavy cream
1 package (15 ounces) cheese tortellini, cooked and drained
2 tablespoons grated Parmesan cheese

In 2-quart saucepan, simmer Ragú Chunky Gardenstyle Pasta Sauce and whipping cream over medium heat, stirring occasionally, 5 minutes or until heated through. Toss hot tortellini with sauce. Sprinkle with cheese and garnish, if desired, with chopped fresh basil. *Makes 4 servings*

Vegetable Almond Fettuccine

Prep and Cook Time: 24 minutes

6 tablespoons butter
2 cloves garlic, minced
2 teaspoons dried basil leaves
1 teaspoon onion powder
¼ teaspoon salt
¼ teaspoon black pepper
1 package (9 ounces) fresh
   spinach fettuccine
¾ pound yellow crookneck squash,
   thinly sliced
1 red bell pepper, coarsely chopped
⅔ cup slivered almonds
¼ cup grated Parmesan cheese

1. Melt butter in small nonstick skillet over high heat. Add garlic; reduce heat. Cook 1 minute. Remove from heat; stir in basil, onion powder, salt and black pepper. Keep warm.

2. Bring 3 quarts water to a boil in large saucepan. Add fettuccine, squash and bell pepper. Cook 3 minutes or until vegetables are crisp-tender. Drain; return to saucepan.

3. Pour butter sauce and almonds over fettuccine; toss. Transfer to serving bowl.

4. Sprinkle with cheese. Serve immediately.

Makes 3 to 4 servings

Fiesta Broccoli, Rice and Beans

Prep and Cook Time: 20 minutes

2 cups frozen broccoli florets
2 cups uncooked instant rice
½ teaspoon chili powder
1 cup salsa or picante sauce
1 can (about 15 ounces) black
   beans, rinsed and drained
¼ cup (1 ounce) shredded Cheddar
   or pepper-Jack cheese

1. Place broccoli and 2 tablespoons water in microwavable dish. Cover loosely with plastic wrap; cook at HIGH 4 to 5 minutes or until crisp-tender.

2. Cook rice according to package directions, adding chili powder to cooking water.

3. Stir salsa and black beans into hot cooked rice. Top each serving of rice and beans with broccoli and cheese.

Makes 4 servings

Pasta Primavera

Prep and Cook Time: 30 minutes

8 ounces uncooked mafalde* pasta
2 medium zucchini (about 1 pound)
3 tablespoons roasted garlic-
     flavored vegetable oil
1 red bell pepper, thinly sliced
½ cup loosely packed fresh basil
     leaves, coarsely chopped
Salt and black pepper to taste
½ cup grated Parmesan cheese

*Broad, flat, ripple-edged
noodles. Fettuccini can be
substituted.*

1. Cook pasta according to package directions; drain. Place in large bowl.

2. While pasta is cooking, cut zucchini lengthwise into halves. Cut crosswise into thin slices.

3. Heat oil in large skillet over medium-high heat until hot. Add zucchini and bell pepper; cook 3 to 4 minutes until vegetables are crisp-tender, stirring frequently.

4. Add zucchini mixture and basil to pasta; toss gently until well combined. Season with salt and black pepper. Serve with cheese.

Makes 4 servings

Quick Skillet Rice Gratin

Prep and Cook Time: 15 minutes

2 tablespoons olive oil
1 onion, chopped
2 cloves garlic, minced
2 medium carrots, peeled and
     chopped
1 teaspoon dried thyme leaves
2 cups uncooked instant white rice
1 can (15½ ounces) kidney beans,
     rinsed and drained
1 teaspoon salt
     Black pepper to taste
⅓ cup grated Parmesan cheese

1. Heat oil in large skillet over medium-high heat until hot. Add onion and garlic; cook and stir 2 minutes. Add carrots and thyme; cook and stir 4 minutes more.

2. Add rice, 2 cups water, beans, salt and pepper. Stir well. Bring to a boil. Reduce heat to low. Sprinkle with cheese. Cover and simmer 5 minutes or until cheese has melted and all liquid has evaporated.

Makes 4 to 6 servings

Cheesy Herb-Stuffed Mushrooms with Spinach Fettuccine

Prep and Cook Time: 30 minutes

2 packages (9 ounces each) fresh spinach fettuccine

⅓ cup extra-virgin olive oil

1 tablespoon dried basil leaves

2 cloves garlic, minced

1 package (6½ ounces) garlic-and-herb spreadable cheese

16 large mushrooms, 2-inch diameter, rinsed and stems removed

1. Prepare grill for direct cooking.

2. Cook fettuccine according to package directions. Drain; return to saucepan.

3. Meanwhile, combine oil, basil and garlic in small bowl; pour over cooked pasta. Toss well; set aside.

4. Cut aluminum foil into 4 large squares. Spoon about 1 tablespoon cheese into each mushroom cap. Place four mushroom caps, cheese side up, in center of each square. Fold aluminum foil to close, leaving small air pocket directly above cheese.

5. Place packets on grid. Grill over hot coals 5 minutes or until mushroom caps are fork-tender. Remove from grill.

6. Transfer fettuccine to serving bowl. Remove mushroom caps from packets; arrange over fettuccine. Serve immediately.

Makes 4 to 6 servings

Serving Suggestion: Grill zucchini spears along with the mushroom packets. Serve with a colorful garden salad and crusty French bread.

The publisher would like to thank the companies and organizations listed below for the use of their recipes and photographs in this publication.

Alaska Seafood Marketing Institute

Birds Eye® Foods

Butterball® Turkey

Del Monte Corporation

Dole Food Company, Inc.

The Golden Grain Company®

Hormel Foods, LLC

Jennie-O Turkey Store®

Lawry's® Foods

National Pork Board

Reckitt Benckiser Inc.

StarKist Seafood Company

Unilever Foods North America

METRIC CONVERSION CHART

VOLUME MEASUREMENTS (dry)

1/8 teaspoon = 0.5 mL
1/4 teaspoon = 1 mL
1/2 teaspoon = 2 mL
3/4 teaspoon = 4 mL
1 teaspoon = 5 mL
1 tablespoon = 15 mL
2 tablespoons = 30 mL
1/4 cup = 60 mL
1/3 cup = 75 mL
1/2 cup = 125 mL
2/3 cup = 150 mL
3/4 cup = 175 mL
1 cup = 250 mL
2 cups = 1 pint = 500 mL
3 cups = 750 mL
4 cups = 1 quart = 1 L

VOLUME MEASUREMENTS (fluid)

1 fluid ounce (2 tablespoons) = 30 mL
4 fluid ounces (1/2 cup) = 125 mL
8 fluid ounces (1 cup) = 250 mL
12 fluid ounces (1 1/2 cups) = 375 mL
16 fluid ounces (2 cups) = 500 mL

WEIGHTS (mass)

1/2 ounce = 15 g
1 ounce = 30 g
3 ounces = 90 g
4 ounces = 120 g
8 ounces = 225 g
10 ounces = 285 g
12 ounces = 360 g
16 ounces = 1 pound = 450 g

DIMENSIONS

1/16 inch = 2 mm
1/8 inch = 3 mm
1/4 inch = 6 mm
1/2 inch = 1.5 cm
3/4 inch = 2 cm
1 inch = 2.5 cm

OVEN TEMPERATURES

250°F = 120°C
275°F = 140°C
300°F = 150°C
325°F = 160°C
350°F = 180°C
375°F = 190°C
400°F = 200°C
425°F = 220°C
450°F = 230°C

BAKING PAN SIZES

Utensil	Size in Inches/Quarts	Metric Volume	Size in Centimeters
Baking or	8×8×2	2 L	20×20×5
Cake Pan	9×9×2	2.5 L	23×23×5
(square or	12×8×2	3 L	30×20×5
rectangular)	13×9×2	3.5 L	33×23×5
Loaf Pan	8×4×3	1.5 L	20×10×7
	9×5×3	2 L	23×13×7
Round Layer	8×1½	1.2 L	20×4
Cake Pan	9×1½	1.5 L	23×4
Pie Plate	8×1¼	750 mL	20×3
	9×1¼	1 L	23×3
Baking Dish	1 quart	1 L	—
or Casserole	1½ quart	1.5 L	—
	2 quart	2 L	—